Am a NoOne!!

My Journey to Everywhere

AUTHOR NAME

Rayan

Made with ❤ on the Notion Press Platform

www.notionpress.com

Contents

Foreword

This is the first book written by the author and he hopes it to do well. This story is a library of experiences of the life of Rayan. A life which has taken very close to experience almost everything but have left him with no identity to be shown as someone big. Story covers different phases of his life and includes sweet, sour and bitter happenings which shaped his life to be able to present himself in the book.

Name of the author of the Foreword : Anonymous

Credentials: SS

Date: 29-Jan-2024

Preface

This book is all written with the experiences and situations of my life explaining how lost someone would feel even after doing a lot of things. I hope my first book would put a smile on the readers face.

Author name: Rayan

Date:29-Jan-2024

Acknowledgments

I would love to acknowledge all the people who were involved in my success and failures and I mention failures because even they give us a lot of things atleast to have them in memories

Am a NoOne!!

Hi!!!

I am **Rayan**... I know am not a very good writer or great with English. But I think we Indians are ok with broken English :D. So here I am sitting in my couch and writing this book to let you know the events that have happened in my 33 years of life which made me think to some extent that.

"Am a NoOne!!"

So, let's start with the year 1991, you know how amazing those days were. I was born in the evening of 26th April 1991 as per the Medical Records. Wait!! as per the medical records!! Yes, cos none of the family members were interested to note down the time or date as they were going through their own Crisis. Why should we go into the details of the crisis as this story is not about that? Am I right? My Father was an Employee of state Govt working as a teacher. Mom was a housewife as it was with most of us back then in 90's.

The day on which I was born my parents were very happy, like all of them use to wish for a baby boy in those days back then. I wish I was a girl though! Let's cut this discussion here cos I don't think I have anything to remember when I was a toddler :P. So, I would start from my schooling days. I think I was in my 4th class when I really started learning thigs about life. Until then I was just a kid with no knowledge about what is life.

My father who was a teacher was good with his students in training them to face the challenges in the future. But with me you know as usual as any other home, he was very nice, and I must say he never hit me or punished me in my whole life. About my mother exactly opposite. I was a very energetic kid. But my mom never used to allow me to go out of our main gate.

As my father was a teacher working in a Government Institution, we had a privilege of staying in the government quarters and I must say it was a super cool community. We had grounds, recreation clubs, dance classes, tennis academies, badminton courts, football classes ohh Hoh Hoh! let me stop it here or else all of you might feel like I was a kid with all the amenities to achieve bigger things in life.

You remember I said I was not allowed to go out so there ends the scene of games and other stuff. And have to say the place was very good, but it was amidst the thick reserve forests in India and that is Nallamala which is spread over five districts in the state. And the school I used to attend was a pretty good one. But all I hate was the Tuition hours or study hours in the Morning and Evening. We used to wake up by 5:30 AM in the morning and walk alongside our father to reach the school by 6:00 AM for the study hours. The tuitions used to end by 8:00 AM and we used to rush back home to get ready for the school.

Thanks to my mom cos only thing that used to fill energy in me was the breakfast. Hot chapatis along with some dal or curry, or Idli and Dosa. Have to say I miss those days, whereas now we don't even have time to have our breakfast properly with busy corporate life's. Oops! Sorry I revealed that I am a corporate employee too soon :P. That's the problem if you get emotional about your past.

Our school as any other school in India used to start with a Mathematics class saying that we have fresh brains in the Mornings and very good to understand, learn and remember. I don't believe in this Idea, and I hate Mathematics where someone says let's say x=a and a= some other crap. I think you got to know about my knowledge in math's with the above example and I am that bad with it. And for that reason, I think my math's teacher used to hate me. Only thing I would listen from him every time he asks me a question and as you can guess I will be wrong with the answer, and he starts saying **"Pandita putra parama sunta"** which translates to *"being a teacher's son why are you so dumb".*

There he had planted a seed in my brain saying that I am good for nothing :P. That's the first one though and there are many more to go. So, the afternoons were again good as my mom used to get acarrier lunch for us every day where my friends used to get a packed box from their home kept in their school bags from morning. Ohhh!! God, I forgot to say about my sister… and here comes the angel of my life my elder sister. You know why she came after a page in my story. Lunch time was the only time she used to irritate me by sharing the food from a box where my mom used to hand feed us. And to be frank let me tell you all, no chef in the world can beat the taste of the food prepared and hand fed by mom. I also used to enjoy the looks of my friend's :P cos none of their moms used to come daily in the lunch time.

Have to say food has always been a great part of my life. Whenever I am sad or mad about something food is the thing that gets me back to normal. Anyways we are into food now will take a small space of my book to say about it. My mom used to prepare the best dal I would say and serve it onto the plate hot along with rice with some ghee on it and there is a taste maker as well added into it that's a pickle of mango or tomato. I know you must be craving for some good food now; ok Iwill stop it here.

There were few times when I can count on my fingers until my 4th class that my mom doesn't showup in the lunch break and have sent the box with some neighbor or with someone else who stays near to my home. And that's when my sister used to have a problem with eating her food. I used to hand feed her even though I was younger than her in age :P. Have to say I would never forget that moments in my life even after 22 years now. There are few things that always stay in your heart no matter what happens in life.

I must say that schooling days are the best days of one's life.

I used to wait for Sundays as that was the only day, I used to wake up happy by 6:30 AM and you know what I had freedom for 2-3 hours after that cos I was enrolled for football coaching on Sundays by my dad. I was a king of my own world on Sundays. I used to walk alongside my dad until we reach the ground and leave his hand and run into the ground once I get the sight of the ground. I used to play and drain enough energy that was stored in me for the whole week.

This was the life every kid would envy till my 4th class.

2. New World

As we are all on a tour to my school days, I remember a small incident. Like any other afternoon wefinished school and as usual me and my sister were walking out of the main entrance of our school to go home. My dad was not at home from couple of days and we thought he would have gone to city on some work for his usual trainings or office work. As we walk out of the gate, we saw ***a new bike (Suzuki Samurai)*** which was shining like a diamond and my dad was sitting on the rider's seat. To be frank I thought I was dreaming. I won't say much but my dad was handsome enough when he was in his 30's. Trust me I use some of his poses even now to showoff :P. And the moment I saw him on a bike I would say the picture got captured in my mind forever and he was looking like a south Indian hero, and he is a hero for me now as well not only the mannerisms but also due to his character the way he cares about people around him.

I ran in a very excited manner as any kid would do after seeing his/her dad after missing him for a couple of days. There he holds me and lift me up and giving me a nice kiss on my cheeks and there follow my sister who runs and holds him very tight and he was very happy to see us. He says pointing at the bike "This is what I have got for you guys being away from town for couple of days". Gotta say this no matter how many bikes or cars we have bought in the future I never forget this bike.

You know right its always precious and never forgotten when it is the first thing someone have bought in the family.

I have stepped into a new world now. I would say this is where I started learning about life. My parents have decided to send me into a boarding school for betterment. I have never been to a city until then. My admission to the boarding school was done immediately once the summer vacations started. I know that once the vacations are completed, I will not have my parents and sister around me every day. That was a vacation in which was shorter than any other.

Finally, the day has arrived where I must leave for the boarding school. No doubt that my parents have made the best arrangements for me over there. But thoughts of not waking up to my dad's voice and my mom getting us ready for the school and fight with my sister while getting ready for school about the socks cos I use to maintain them bad and use to take my sisters every day :P and, Ihate to polish my shoes, how would I live without all these things every day in the morning.

My dad as any other got my packed bags near to the main door and said, I think we need to leave now, we may miss the bus or else. I know it's quite filmy. My home we never experienced being far from each other, so hugs and blessings were new :P. After these obligatory things I took my backpack and sat inside the auto which my dad booked to drop us in the bus station.

Trust me this was the shortest journey I have ever been on a bus, 9 hours felt as if they flew off in seconds.

After reaching the city, my fathers' friend had come to pick up and drop us at the boarding school. As we get into his car and start driving towards the school, he asks me *"How are you Beta?"*, I was not even listening to him as I was scared to stay alone at a new place. I answered, *'I am ok uncle'* and it satisfied him. My dad and his friend were talking about the things that happened since they last met. I heard my dad saying that the school is 25 kms away from the city bus station. I thought I had time but think about it when a 9-hour journey seemed to be just seconds, 25 kms is nothing.

Here we reach the school premises. There was a huge gate may be a 15–20-footer and a compound wall of about 15 feet. As we reach the gate and park the car the security personnel over there opened a small gate which was also a part of the big gate. Now I entered the premises to my surprise I see all the children playing in the ground. And let me tell you the campus was a feast.There was a basketball court which looked like the one we see on TV where the NBA players play. Right after that there was a volleyball court. And besides that, there were 4 nets to practice cricket. As my eyes feast on these things a guy came near to us saying the principal is ready to meet you.

I was not even listening to the discussion there between my dad and the principal. I was just looking out from the window seeing all the kids enjoying there in the ground. So now I was ready to stay there as no one would stop me from playing in the ground now. The principal had asked the office boy to give us a tour of campus and I started liking the place slowly as the tour finishes. Now comes the odd situation where my dad is leaving my things in a hostel room full of bunker beds. He saw me and asked me whether everything's fine. He did a last inspection whether I have all the basic things to survive in a hostel.

There comes a warden to take handover of me from my father. And my father signed a paper andthere starts a new journey in my life. I remember even now when my dad went out of that main gate and waved me from outside. Obvious that I was crying but you know what the events next are going to get pretty much exciting.

3. The Rise to Fame

Lots of noises in the ground behind the main gate. Too many voices raise to welcome a team. Lots of Hip! Hip! Hurrahs! Everyone is happy in the school as the team won a District Volleyball Tournament. To the applause of all the students the main gates open and the team gets into the school in a bus. A boy who is not more than 5 feet 4 inches get out of the bus along with a trophy in his hands. And hand it over to the principal and people lift him up on their shoulders in joy as if he is a hero. And he becomes the School People Leader (SPL).

Let me tell you all that this was not me, Ha ha ha. It was a student from 10th class. But the thing is I was very inspired seeing that being a student of 5th class and I always wanted to reach that position. So, after a long wait we had selections for volleyball juniors' team in the school when I was in 8th class. Anyone would obviously guess now where I would be after knowing this. Yes, I landed up on the court even before the actual process of selection started :P.

The coach at my school was a national player twice and assistant coach to National Volleyball team for 5 years. Now we all stand in front of him to face a ball out of his hands and just wish that the ball reaches back to him in the position he is standing. I was the last one in the queue due to nervousness even after reaching earlier than anyone else in my class. Here comes the decider, I was in front of the coach, and he throws ball at me and guess what! :D Ha ha ha, I have played the ball miles away from the coach.

Reaction I think we all know; the coach had asked me to leave the court. There were 2 months left for the final exams of my 8th class and we were all busy with the preparations. But I used to wake up by 5:30 in the morning so that I don't miss to see the champions playing the game of volleyball in the court. I used to envy the way the champ plays i.e., the ***"SPL (The Boy with a trophy from the bus)".*** Final exams have finished and in comes the most awaited summer vacation and we all pack our bags to home and meet our loved ones and spend quality time for a month and half.

My Dad was at the school to pick me up. I got into the auto towards the bus station. The first word from me to my dad was ***"I want to play Volleyball".*** He said why not didn't you enroll in your school team? I said the coach said I am not a fit cos I couldn't play a ball right back to him in the selection. My dad didn't say anything, but he stopped the auto rickshaw in front of a sports shop to buy me a pair of volleyball shoes. I remember my dad saying that day who is he to stop you, I will get you a ball as well let's start practice in the summer at home.

I never knew that my dad was a champion himself and played in state team from his college. Now you see may be that's where volleyball dragged me into it. The summer finished and I was back to school in 9th class. I used to wake up by 5:30 Am every morning and wear the shoes and go out for ajog and play along side lines. The luck came my way when we sideliners got a chance to play along with the senior team. And luckily the coach was part of the team I was playing in. I have received two difficult balls and placed them to get points for the team which Impressed my coach.

After that I won't say much about this because this story is not about a sport, but it is about **"NoOne"** among and in us. I went onto win the district volleyball tournament and have also become the "***SPL (Same as the Boy who walked out of the bus with a trophy :P)".*** I also got selected into the national team after that.

I would say I have Risen to the fame with the inspiration from one of my seniors. But do not forget this is the story of a **NoOne!!!** I would like to end this part with an amazing quote from a late singer, songwriter and musician "***You never know how strong you are until being strong is the only choice you have"*** 😊 – ***"Bob Marley"*** so to achieve my goal I had to be strong, and I did it.

4. The Love Letter

It was a fine morning where the assembly of the school people starts with a prayer. Prayer is organized always by the school people leader. That was my first assembly after the Tournament. As usual the Parade starts with a school band and continues with the National Anthem, Headlines of the news, few good words from the principal, then ends up with a march fast to respective classes. That day was different. Once the newspaper reading part is done Principal had asked me to step onto the stage and holds me on my shoulders and praises me for the game I have played in the tournament.

I should say this is the moment anyone of us would envy when we were in school. There was an applause from almost 800 students, and you can understand how that would make you feel □. Trust me I was not a **"NoOne"** there. My principal after his words hugged me and was very happy that our schools name is on top in the district due to the win and there was an article about that written on one of a leading newspaper those days. I remember my dad received a letter of appreciation at home for the achievements and my mom called me and she was so happy that they took the next bus to the city to meet me on the weekend. You can guess I had a feast of mom made sweets and snacks □.

My school had strict teachers as well and you can guess who would punish me more often and for obvious reasons that was my Mathematics teacher :P. I was kneed down in front of my class as I could not solve a problem given to me along with one of my friends in my class who was almost touching my level of intelligence in Math's :P. As we kneed down, we started some funny discussion and were laughing looking at each other. This guy I am tagged along with on punishment was a funny animal. Even his face use to tickle me :P.

Right behind his tickling face I see a group of girls walking out from the 9th class who are my juniors. You know what I asked him to shut his mouth as they pass us so that they don't laugh at us being punished. A girl from the group pointed at us and whispered something and that made everyone in the group laugh at us. But I see one of the girls from the group stopping them and you know what no matter what's your age we can understand the power of eye contact.

We have all experienced that moment when you look into someone's eyes and see a million unspoken words. Simply having someone stare back at you could make you all sweaty. Moreover, this was my first time and my eyes unknowingly turned down onto the floor as I was scared. I must say here as a matured individual now, we don't have to believe in love at first sight, to appreciate the power of eye contact. Simply meeting eyes with someone won't make them fall head over heels for you, but it sure will do many other things that can turn them from a “maybe” to a “yes”.

Trust me I was a very shy kid and, I should tell you about our vice principal. He was 6 feet tall and handsome mid 40’s man. The whole school used to fear him cos he never even gives a smile, and he maintains his stature. I remember him coming to our class in study hours once knowing one of the students in my class proposed his love to some girl and trust me the bamboo stick, he got along with him broken the way he beat the hell out of him. After that none of us ever dared looking at a girl. You remember the reaction of my eyes unknowingly turned down onto the floor, I would say that was knowingly due to the fear :P.

I remember this girl staring at me whenever she passes from our classroom, and I used to behave as if I am not looking at her. Half-Yearly exams were about to start where we used to sit along with the juniors beside us so that there is no cheating. And we were all excited about the exams as we get a vacation of 10 days right after that. Once the exams were finished I landed up for the vacations in the newly bought home by my dad in the city.

I wake up to my mom’s voice on a fine morning instead of dads in the vacation and she gives me the mobile saying some girl from you class is calling you regarding some assignment. I was shell shocked that I never talk to a girl in my class and who the hell it would be. I took the phone and it was a sweet voice saying I am **Zoya** from 9th class. You know what my reaction was, I jumped out of my bed and ran onto the terrace and my first question to her was how you know the number of my home. She said your friend gave me, he was sitting beside me in the exam.

Trust me this was all new for me at home and that too I was just a 14-year-old kid. I quickly disconnected the call saying talk to me in the school. My mom was asking me why you ran onto the terrace and what did you speak, and she was pulling my legs saying is she your girlfriend. I told don't even think about it my Vice Principal will tear me into pieces. So, the vacation ended, and we were back to school. First thing I did was confront my friend what was the reason for giving my home contact number to her and asked whether anyone else know about this other than him. He said "No" and it was a breather for me.

As usual the assembly finished, and all the students were marching towards the classes. I was standing on the stairs to see if the people are following the queue. There comes **Zoya** with a smile on her face. Trust me my heartbeat was almost touching the speed of a Bugatti on its highs. And she takes her hand out of her pocket and gives me a nicely decorated and folded piece of paper. As if I was expecting it from her, I also took the paper and immediately shoved it into my pocket so that no one can see. You all see this is what I was talking about the power of eye contact and you can see a million unspoken words.

So here the scenario changed from **No eye contact** to **Glance** then **The Gaze** and **The Smile**... And don't forget about ***"The Dream Boat"*** I am going to board after all this… and a **boat anchor** which is stuck; :P that's my vice principal I see him coming down from the stairs in front of me and the Boat is broken… :P

5. The Interview

I landed finally in the silicon city in the search of a job after completing my Graduation. I was lucky enough that my elder sister was staying in the city for 5 years and she had a place already where I could stay. She was a HR, so I had a mentor as well for my Job search. She helped me with creating my profile, CV's, trained me about the corporate etiquettes and also how to attend an interview and all these were new to me. But you never know where you are going to end up no matter what your life was in past.

I started giving interview 's for Marketing positions as I was trying for a field job because sitting in a cubicle was never my plan. Gave more than 8-9 interviews without any success in 3 months. I was frustrated and didn't want to waste any more time. Decided to pursue MBA as everyone usually does if you don't get a job just get yourself enrolled for post graduate program :P. I started going for a coaching to attend the entrance exam for admissions. Right after a couple of days in training I received a mail from one of the corporate companies saying they would like to discuss on my candidature.

So now let me tell you something, no matter whatever you plan and wherever you wanna see yourself in future, I don't think that's a cake walk for everyone. At least for a "**NoOne**" like me. I don't say that there are no one who have achieved what they wanted to be in life. It all depends on the situations and support you get. That's a lot of philosophy :P. Let's move on.

I think all of you have guessed right and I have reached the office for the discussion with document holder and a bag full of documents fully dressed in formals and neatly combed which I never use to. The receptionist has asked me to wait in the lobby until the manager of the project I would be selected gets free for the discussion. Must tell you all, this was the second time I was in this office. The first day when I attended the interview the HR over there made me wait on the couch in the lobby for almost 4 hours. My sister who is a HR suggested me to sit very steady when you are waiting to go in for the interview. Now you can Imagine how is the situation. I was sitting on a couch continuously for 4 hours steadily without even knowing where the restroom is and was shy in asking anyone out there in the reception.

For the second time I was lucky the manager asked me to meet him in just 15 min :P. Have to say he was a very cool middle-aged guy. That was coolest interview I have ever been on, in my whole life. Believe it or not I got the Job, but a cubicle one

One fine day in my life I had to start a job with a tag in my neck and living my life according to the timings given by the org. Basically, you are no one to decide when you are willing to eat or drink or take a vacation. You need to wait for the weekend to call your friends and talk to them freely for an hour. You must wait for the weekend to go and watch a movie of your favorite hero and not on the release day. Most importantly you would do all those things which are not good for your health such as no work outs, no peace, no sleep, no proper food, no sports, losing all your friends slowly, lots of corporate politics, Rat Race to be a winner/leader/performer of the year/people manager and what not.

It's been 10 years now that I have been in the corporate world working with 6 different companies and the first company was the one, I worked for longest. Not because it was only good one, again it was also because people said, *"you have to work more than a couple of years in the company you start with to show your stability". Post that I have switched at least one company in one and half years in search of stability in my life but not on my resume.*

I am in a good position in life working for more than10 years for different organizations, but I am missing many things in life which had left me at a point now thinking "**Am a NoOne!!".**

Another gem of a quote from an American Poet ***"To be nobody but yourself in a world that's doing***

its best to make you somebody else is to fight the hardest battle you are ever going to fight.Never stop fighting" – E.E. Cummings.

6. The Reckless Soul

Finish line is set for an 8 kms running race. A guy is waving the finishing flag, and there comes the participants. There are 3 well-built boys running very fast to finish the race on top. There is one more lean 5 feet 6 inches boy who is running behind them to be on top. And that was me. I finished4th in the race qualifying to get a seat in a Defense academy when I was 15 years old. I always dreamed of being a defense pilot. I have put in all off my efforts to be there by training myself and playing a lot of sports.

Getting into a defense college is not that easy and you need to be good with Mathematics too, to be able to qualify. I somehow managed to cross the line being the 4th one to be qualified to get into the college. Trust me that was one hell of struggle □. The day came when I was ready to shift to the defense college. I see my mom and dad discussing very seriously that day while my dad was ready to drop me. I was only thinking of being a non-technical pilot and I was already working on some Airbase.

Here comes my dad, and he says you are not joining the defense academy. I asked him why dad. Because your mom doesn't want her only son to be in defense. The thing is I had million words to say but was silent. That silence had killed my dream. It took me 5-6 years to understand the silence. ***"When your parents are not so rich but if they are still trying to give you beautiful life by sacrificing their own happiness***" - I think the silence comes out of that appreciation to respect their words. But my journey to be a **NoOne** started here.

I think parents can do anything for their kids/children except allowing them to be themselves. I was sent to a Boarding college to complete my Intermediate in Life sciences background. The college was chosen because my sister completed her intermediate there. And it was a town far away from the city. Now I was used to my friends from different places and to the city environment.

Suddenly, I was sent to a college where it was totally the opposite to my school. The hostel rooms were not clean, and the washrooms don't even think of stepping into them. And my first day to the study hours everyone was laughing at me cos I was wearing shorts. Rest of the students were wearing Lungi's and cotton pants. To my surprise one of the faculty even mocked me saying that looks like a joker's costume.

The dining hall was not even close to a desi dhaba. The serving guys over there use to sweep the hall and serve the food without even washing their hands. Now let me tell you I visited the dining hall to eat the food for 4 times in the entire year. And the result of my 1st year was amazing I only passed English and Sanskrit Languages and failed in all the other subjects. I was at home for the holidays before my 2nd year started. And my parents decided to get me back to the city for my 2nd year.

It was a breather for me, and I am back to the city. Where I had to pass in all the 4 subjects which were left in the first year along with the 2nd year subjects. But along with these my circle of friends grew a lot gradually taking me towards the student's politics. I had very nice bunch of friends who always supported me throughout these years which made me rise to a very good position where I was to be the person to reach out to when you have a fight or some settlement in the college and also outside in the political circles.

The college I was enrolled to was the epicenter of the student politics in the city. And I was elected as the prime representative of a student wing of a political party from my college. As our college was very important for the political parties and its members to get the crowd for their events we were always in demand. Me and a couple of friends from the college were in constant touch with the MLA (Member of legislative assembly) or I would say vice versa for organizing the upcoming party activities and rallies.

This was the time I grew up being a leader to the masses. In no time I was a very close aide to the MLA. I always used to be surrounded by a group of students and friends discussing the prospects of the future events. In no time people started recognizing me by my name and the political party I work for. When I say people, it also includes the govt officials and police. At this point of time, I was flying very **"Reckless"** not thinking of what I would go through in the future.

It so happened that people around me have started using my name in order to dodge the police checks. As you grow in politics it is so obvious that you go through many fights and settlements which involves your friends or just for the sake of earning money to be able to keep the people happy who are associated with you. In the process I used to meet the MLA almost every day and was always part of the discussions and decision makings which made him trust me a lot and also due to the following behind me.

Amidst all these I have never thought how ruthless and brainless I have turned. Only good thing I remember was starting an organization to fund the trusts who gave shelter to the old and orphans. We used to collect the funds and organize big events and hand them over to the trusts who help the needy, because of which I appeared on the newspapers and in turn pulling more people towards the political group I was heading.

Property settlements, court cases, fights between two groups, intense fights for girlfriends, getting people out of police station and you name anything which can be called as a non-sense, I was a part of it and leading it. I somehow was able to finish my 2nd year which is also known as +2 in India amidst all the ruckus I was going through and was a part of. No need to say that I have got a lot of support in the examination hall to pass the exams I was appearing. I short I have cheated.

No matter what I was doing outside my home I was always a good kid Infront of my parents. I was able to get a seat into Bachelors in a nearby college from my home. Trust me it was never my plan to pursue a life sciences graduation. This was also a result of my ***"Silence"*** infront of my parents. It was a 4-year course and almost all the staff of the college were known to me as I have met them many a times during the political events and also when they needed help from the student wings of the politics. This gave me the leverage to do whatever I want while I was in college.

I had 8% of attendance throughout the 4 years I have spent in the college. There is a reason I have used the word spent and not studied cos I have never. People always used to find me in the places which we call as our **'adda'** discussing on things to grow more in the politics.

I somehow missed the logic that I am turning into **"The Reckless Soul"** who is not thinking anything about the future and where he is headed towards. It was almost the last semester of my 4 years in the college and I was left with 3 arrears along with the subjects in the final year. As usual as I was well connected to the staff and faculty, because of which I was able to pass the huddle and secure the degree. I think this was the time where my family started pressurizing me to move to another city where my sister have completed her education and is working with an MNC.

Amidst a lot of discussions and fights in the family and with the demand from my sister I had to leave all of those things which I have worked hard to create my empire in the city and moved to an entirely different city with different language and different people.

7. The Responsibility – "Not Given but Taken"

My father always played a vital role in my life, where I have followed many of his words in the journey so far in my life. I always remember him saying **"party hard but only when it's your hard earned money, get a girlfriend or partner when you have earnings to maintain yourself".** To be frank these words always rang in my mind until I got a job. So, I have never thought of partying or having a partner until I was dependent.

The initial year after joining the job, I was very serious about climbing the ladder up and in the process of doing I was unknowingly pulled into a very big league of rat race where millions of professionals are working really hard in India to show up their presence and make an identity for themselves. It was insane to say that I have worked 18 hours in a stretch a day in order to get the so-called appraisals from clients and praising from boss. When I am writing them down now and thinking of those days, I feel I was very foolish the way I have tried being competitive and to be the winning horse in the race.

So here I stand as a mentor for the new joiners after a year and half of giving up my personal space and time to the corporate, thinking I would be a very big man someday. When I recollect those days, I still laugh at my innocence in not seeing the future. Growing up to this stage I was very straight forward and cut throat with all my words and works. By saying this I meant I stand no chance to move up the ladder at the pace others would do with their intelligence to adapt the situation and use their tactics to be in limelight. I would not discuss more on this because it always depends on the individuals whether how they aspiring shape up their own life.

I have been able to onboard more than 20 joiners with my mentoring onto the system making them good contributors towards the company's business. After almost 3 years of journey with the first company I had to resign as I was getting the appraisals over the positions to be the people manager but not monetarily.

I always had a dream of owning a sweet home, and there goes my hunt of getting one when I was 27 years old. To be frank no one in my family did this at this age. My father and my family were very happy with the progress of my life. I always had dissatisfaction on how my life shaped out and the way it is going on.

To the day when I am writing this I always think, whether I have reached my destination where I was thinking that my happiness resides in a peaceful state. Writing this was only a way to satisfy my soul and relive the memories which were sweet, sour and also bitter.

The boat which was broken in my school when I was a ***"School People Leader"*** was due to the "***silence***" out of fear. There were many situations where I gave up on many things due to my silence and society including my parents. The world will never give you a second chance, it is very ruthless. Trust me "***people will try to destroy you, because they recognize your power, that is not because they don't see it, because they see it and don't want it to exist***."

Finally, what I would say is I am living a good life but not the best one. I used to think remaining silent is classy when you have a lot to say, but it never works in this world.

And here I continue be a NoOne with a lot of dreams which I only thinkof fulfilling when I am dreaming.

This is Rayan signing off for now... ☺

Names used in the book are all made up not to let out anyone's identity, but the writings are all real.

www.ingramcontent.com/pod-product-compliance
Lightning Source LLC
LaVergne TN
LVHW041257150826
845673LV00008B/2629

* 9 7 9 8 8 9 2 7 7 1 7 7 1 *